You're SHOPPING ME CRAZY!

101 Discourteous, Inconsiderate, Thoughtless, and Annoying Shopping Situations

John Reinhardt

You're Shopping Me Crazy!

USA edition

Copyright © 2025 by John Reinhardt

All Rights Reserved. No part of this book may be used or reproduced in any form or by any electronic or mechanical means including informational storage or retrieval systems without written permission except in the case of brief quotations embodied in critical articles and reviews.

ISBN: 979-8-9876310-3-4 (Paperback)
ISBN: 979-8-9876310-4-1 (eBook)

For information contact:

John Reinhardt
DesignerofBooks@gmail.com
802-236-4147
youredrivingmecrazy.com

Edited by Kathleen Strattan
Cover illustration by Malane Newman
Cover and text design by John Reinhardt Book Design

Important Notes

While this book focuses primarily on the grocery shopping experience, many of these behaviors we'll explore are not exclusive to this setting, and can be found in stores of varying merchandise.

My suggestions are to assist you in making decisions and supporting a culture of kindness, consideration, respect, and meaning in our everyday lives.

I hope you find this book helpful and entertaining, and that you can relate to these experiences and observations.

Printed in the United States of America

To my wife, Lynn,
and our daughter, Kim

Acknowledgments

First, thank you to all the store owners, managers, and employees who work hard to make our shopping experience enjoyable and efficient.

Thank you to my wife, Lynn, for everything.

Thank you to Kathleen Strattan, whose superior editing, enthusiasm, and support for this project have been priceless.

Thank you to Malane Newman. Her incredible illustration skills are showcased on this book's cover.

Thank you to the following people for their valuable feedback: Jon Strattan, Beth Hollen, Sherri Cheline, Terri Huber, and Teresa Overbeck.

And finally, thank you to all the shoppers out there who helped make this book possible by constantly…

Shopping Me Crazy!

Contents

Important Notes ii
Acknowledgments. v
Introduction. 1
Develop Good Shopping Habits 3
Challenge 5

- ☐ Stopping Short. 7
- ☐ Placing Items on the Belt 8
- ☐ Cramming Items on the Belt 9
- ☐ Bagging 10
- ☐ Waiting for the Total to Find Payment . . 12
- ☐ Price Checks 14
- ☐ Turning Without Looking 15
- ☐ Talking Too Long at Checkout 15
- ☐ Going Back for Something 16
- ☐ Slow Checkout 17
- ☐ Parking Lot Behavior 18
- ☐ Shopping Carts 20
- ☐ Restrooms 22
- ☐ Greetings!. 23
- ☐ Blocking the Aisle 24

CONTENTS

- ☐ Leaving and Entering an Aisle Without Looking 25
- ☐ Eating Unpaid Food While Shopping ... 26
- ☐ Bumping People With the Cart 27
- ☐ Not Putting Items Back Where They Came From 28
- ☐ Children in the Store 28
- ☐ Employees Not Giving the Customer the Right-of-Way 31
- ☐ Leaving Trash in the Cart 32
- ☐ Getting in Front of You While You're Browsing Products 34
- ☐ Pedestrians in the Parking Lot 35
- ☐ Loitering 36
- ☐ Dealing with Deli Line-Cutters 37
- ☐ Littering 38
- ☐ Using an Express Lane With Too Many Items 39
- ☐ Touching Fresh Bakery Items 40
- ☐ Rudeness to Employees 41
- ☐ Being Loud 42
- ☐ Cutting in Line at the Cash Register..... 43
- ☐ On Saying "Thank You" 44
- ☐ Abandoning a Cart 45

CONTENTS

- ☐ People Who Shop Behind You 46
- ☐ Expired Items 47
- ☐ Opening a New Checkout Lane 48
- ☐ Handing the Cashier Trash to Throw Away 49
- ☐ All About the Phone (and Speakerphone) .. 50
- ☐ Employees Rude/Unhelpful to Customers 51
- ☐ Coupons Are Great, But... 52
- ☐ Not Knowing How to Use the Credit Card Swipe 54
- ☐ Freezer Doors 55
- ☐ Throwing Crumpled Bills on the Counter 56
- ☐ Talking on the Phone While Going Through the Checkout 57
- ☐ Dressing in Pajamas 57
- ☐ Licking Fingers to Sort Bills at the Checkout 58
- ☐ Spilled Items Left on the Floor 59
- ☐ An Employee Doesn't Offer Help 60
- ☐ Drivers Not Stopping for Pedestrians at Entrance....................... 61
- ☐ Personal Cleanliness.................. 61

CONTENTS

- ☐ Trash on the Floors 62
- ☐ Rotten Fruit and Vegetables 63
- ☐ No Gridlock at the Checkout, Please!.... 64
- ☐ Handing Items to the Cashier 65
- ☐ Motorized Carts Coming Through ....
  Regardless (and Blocking the Aisles) .. 65
- ☐ Backing Up in the Parking Lot
  Without Looking 66
- ☐ Driving Down the Wrong Direction
  in the Parking Lot 67
- ☐ Not Enough Checkout Lanes Open 68
- ☐ Stealing Slots in the Parking Lot 69
- ☐ Leave Heavy Items in the Cart 70
- ☐ Reaching Over You to Grab Something .. 70
- ☐ Placing a Basket Full of Items
  on the Belt 71
- ☐ Taking Multiple Free Samples
  and Hanging Out at That Spot 72
- ☐ Unruly Pets 72
- ☐ Crowding You at Checkout 73
- ☐ Parking in Handicapped Spaces
  Without a Sticker 74
- ☐ Disregard for Older and Disabled People .. 75
- ☐ Drunk Shoppers 76

CONTENTS

- ☐ Letting Little Kids Push the Cart 77
- ☐ Shoplifters 78
- ☐ Aggressive Charity Stands 79
- ☐ Sampling Fruit, Like Grapes 80
- ☐ Sniffing Fresh Fruit or Vegetables 80
- ☐ No Cleaning Wipes at the Entrance 81
- ☐ Narrow Aisles 82
- ☐ Walking on Both Sides of the Aisles 83
- ☐ Greeting Cards........................ 84
- ☐ Reading Magazines and Newspapers Without Buying 85
- ☐ Store Music Selection, Quality, and Volume 86
- ☐ Employees Smoking by the Entrance ... 87
- ☐ Going In the Exit and Out the Enter Doors 88
- ☐ Customer Service Desk 88
- ☐ Causing a Scene 89
- ☐ Unsolvable Mysteries at the Checkout 90
- ☐ Lousy Intercom System 91
- ☐ Self-Checkout 91
- ☐ Labels Facing Every Which Way........ 92
- ☐ Cashier and Bagger Chatting........... 93

- ☐ Camping Out to Study the Vitamin or OTC Section 94
- ☐ Blocking the Exit or Aisle When Catching Up With an Old Friend 95
- ☐ People Who Are Too Chatty About What You're Buying 96
- ☐ No Money for Groceries 97
- ☐ No Staff at the Bakery—Now What? 98
- ☐ Digital Age Difficulties 99
- ☐ Items Falling Through Gaps in the Cart 100
- ☐ Don't Open Me, Please! 101
- ☐ Shopping While Sick 102
- ☐ Shopping Delivery Services 103
- ☐ Handbaskets 105
- ☐ Closing Time 105

Tips for Courteous and Friendly Shopping 107
Afterword 109
About the Author 111

Introduction

In high school, I took a "Family Living" class, and I believe it was one of the most important classes I ever had. I wish this class were a requirement in every school. The knowledge I gained has served me my entire life in everything I do.

Among the many topics, we learned about family dynamics, social forces, the family life cycle, life lessons. We learned how to use a checkbook and keep a balance. But the one thing I remember most was shopping. We learned about sales, store etiquette, and how to balance desires and needs.

I love to visit grocery stores and find new and local products. I enjoy seeing all the label graphics and packaging. I also believe the grocery store can be a microcosm of our society's attitudes and behaviors. And we can learn a lot about how to behave in public by watching people at the grocery store—both the good and the bad.

This environment is also excellent for teaching children how to act outside the home.

I hope you'll enjoy spotting some familiar situations in the following pages, and that you get to have a few laughs along the way. Most of all, I hope you'll find at least one helpful takeaway that stays with you and comes in handy for the rest of your life.

Develop Good Shopping Habits

All shoppers should demonstrate basic respect, consideration of others and property, and common sense.

Okay, we know what to do, but what do we do when others aren't behaving? While we hope others will uphold our shopping standards, we should always be prepared for the opposite.

This book will help you avoid problems caused by others' thoughtless behaviors and teach you how to keep from doing those things yourself, all while maintaining your sense of humor. Anticipating potential scenarios and creating options will reduce stress.

With these tools, you should be able to enjoy your shopping experience to the fullest.

Let's strive to be better shoppers and do the right thing!

Challenge

As you read through the book, record how many of these topics you see shoppers do, including yourself, by marking the checkboxes before each topic on the Contents page.

After you've read the book, and you know what to look for, challenge your friends to see who can spot the most. Feel free to let me know how many you've seen. There are a lot of them, so I doubt you'll see them all anytime soon. But given time, you might!

Also, if you see any bad shopping habits or situations not mentioned in this book, let me know by emailing me at designerofbooks@gmail.com. I'll make note of them and possibly include them in the next edition and give you credit.

Be sure to check out the book's website at youredrivingmecrazy.com.

Let's Go Shopping!

Stopping Short

Whoa, Nelly! Most stores do a good job of providing a wide-open space at the main entrance. Usually, the carts are right there, and you can quickly enter the store.

But some, after getting their cart and seemingly on their way in, suddenly stop right inside the store to look for their shopping list or phone. This triggers a chain reaction behind them.

And then some do this same thing going down the aisle. These people are obviously in their own world and act as though they're alone in the store. Just when you think they'll get going, they stop again. Come on, let's go!

And wait, if that isn't bad enough, what about the people who storm past you from behind as you wait patiently for the person in front of you to move?

Of course, Murphy's Law says you're sure to run into these same people again at the deli counter or checkout line.

Get out your list and phone and whatever else you need before entering the store, please. Likewise, if you want to wipe the handle of your cart before entering the store (always a good idea). Or if you need to come in out of the wind or rain first, step off to the side, out of the way of shoppers behind you.

Placing Items on the Belt

Here's an idea to help you and the bagger. When placing your items on the belt, try to group items from heavy to light and warm to cold. This not only aids the bagging process but also sets up your bags for a more organized unpacking at home.

For example, start with soda and beer, then move on to canned and boxed items, followed by lighter non-refrigerated items, warm items if you have any, and finally cold, frozen, and crushable items.

Are you buying multiples of the same thing—say, four identical jars of applesauce? It helps things go faster if you group them so the cashier can count them, scan one item, and press 4—instead of scanning each identical item separately if they're randomly peppered throughout all your items on the belt. Or you can put one of the four items on the belt and tell the cashier you have four of those items. This eliminates the need to put all of them on the belt and then all of them back in the cart. Saves time and energy.

I always keep a couple of soft cooler bags in the car for added convenience. Maybe you do this, too. These bags are perfect for keeping cold and frozen items from thawing during my trip home. (See also "Bagging.")

101 SHOPPING SITUATIONS

Cramming Items on the Belt

Hurry! Hurry! Get your stuff on the belt NOW! There you are, casually placing your items on the conveyor as the person in front of you continues to have their items scanned. You empty your cart and politely place the separator bar behind the last of your items. Six to eight inches of space may be left on the belt, and the person behind you begins placing their items on the belt.

All is good, right? Nope. You get that person who must put everything they can in that available space. They can't wait!

Watch as they try to fit as many items in the space as possible, stacking them three or four high. And as the belt inches forward, they continue to stack more of their items in the newly created space. And some will even glare at you if you have your items spaced out.

Remember, it's not a race to empty your cart. Nobody's going to swoop in and take your space. Your turn is next. It's okay. Just take a deep breath and chill out!

Bagging

Sure, put the hot fried chicken in with the ice cream! How many times have you had cold items bagged with warm? Or the bag is too heavy and breaks when you lift it? And the classic situation of bread placed at the bottom of the bag? And what's the deal with the cheap, thin plastic bags that tear apart or split when you take them out of the cart?

Some cashiers will bag as they scan. Very efficient. Others slide everything down to the end of the counter and will only bag after the transaction is complete.

You can tell a lot about a person's personality when they bag groceries. I love it when that person has a conversation with me. And I can thank them for the job well done.

You'll occasionally encounter the bagger who has their mind on everything but the task at hand. They're in no hurry. They still have five hours in their shift to kill.

Or they're having a conversation with the cashier and not engaging with the customer. They may be discussing their previous or upcoming weekend, or some other personal matter the customer really doesn't want to hear. (See also "Cashier and Bagger Chatting.")

And then you have situations where there's no one to bag. What do you do? I bag. I prefer to bag. I suggest you offer to bag your own. It's not only faster, but you also get everything bagged exactly the way you want. Plus, it's a great way to ensure your groceries are handled with care and to practice your bagging skills.

The cashier might appreciate it, too—a win-win.

Bagging isn't rocket science, but it does require a certain level of awareness and organizational skills.

I think every store employee should undergo a mandatory week of bagging training—though I realize the class would only need to be about fifteen seconds for a quick study like you. Well, you can take my 39-second class right here:

Bagging 101:

- Ask if the customer prefers paper or plastic bags.
- Don't put cold items with warm items.
- Don't put non-food items with food items.
- Keep vegetables together. Keep frozen foods in separate bags.
- Raw meat is bagged separately.
- Double-bag heavy items.
- Place like item bags together in the cart.

- Heavy stuff on the bottom, light and fragile items on top.
- Always ask if the customer wants the gum, candy, soda, greeting cards, etc., left out or put in their own bags.
- Keep the bags light for easy lifting to prevent them from breaking.
- If items are on the bottom tray of the cart, remind the customer so they're not forgotten.
- If the store allows, offer to help load the bags into the customer's car.
- When finished, thank the customer, and wish them a nice day.

It's easy! And, as I always say, if you take pride in doing small stuff, you're building character for when you're tasked with important stuff.
(See also "Placing Items on the Belt.")

Waiting for the Total to Find Payment

What was that amount again? I think I might have the exact change. Remember the days when cash or a check was the norm? I'm sure we've all been stuck behind someone—or have been this person—who waits until the cashier has registered every item before they begin searching through their purse or pocket for their checkbook or cash.

And then, to make matters worse, they'll first ask for a pen, and then write slowly, dig for their identification, and then ask again for the amount—or take time to count out the exact change in pennies—while holding up an ever-lengthening line. Then, once they hand the cashier their payment, they take their sweet time putting everything away. Yikes!

These days, with scanning bar codes, credit card machines (most with the tap feature now), and easy-to-use rewards cards, you'd think we would have reduced or even eliminated that unnecessary wait time.

But no…there are still people out there who stand there and watch every item being scanned before even beginning to think about getting their payment ready.

All it takes to avoid being this person is the good habit of having everything you need for payment ready before you reach the cashier. Planning ahead is an easy way to respect others' time (your own time, too), and as a bonus, your ice cream might still be frozen when you get home.

Price Checks

"I need someone to go on a hunting expedition for the price of this, please?" I sometimes find myself behind someone who has one or more items with no price or barcode. We all have to wait for the cashier to call for help, then wait for an employee to come to the register, and finally, go out and find the item in the store.

With barcodes on everything today, this situation isn't as common as it used to be, but it still happens. Some barcodes are ripped, marred, wrinkled, not in the system, or even missing.

Before scanners, every item had a price tag—and if the price tag was missing, a not-uncommon occurrence, I recall cashiers occasionally just throwing in a price, as long as it was agreeable to the customer.

Back then, I always checked to ensure a price tag was on an item before putting it in my cart. And I still do this, checking for intact bar codes. I have to admit I have a low level of OCD (obsessive-compulsive disorder), so it's my nature. While I invite you to join me in doing this, I don't insist. But think about it this way—you'll never be the one holding up the line for a price check.

.

Turning Without Looking

Oops, sorry! Has this ever happened to you? The person in front of you is walking along, and then suddenly, without warning, they decide to go back, turn around, and walk right into you.

This happens in a store when someone is stopped and you attempt to go by them. That's when they decide to turn around and slam their cart into yours, or you if you don't have a cart.

And they're unaware they've caused any kind of problem. Sheesh! I sometimes wonder if I'm surrounded by zombies, unaware of everything around them.

It wouldn't hurt to navigate your cart the way you drive your car—you'd never swing your car around without first looking to make sure you won't crash into someone behind you.

Talking Too Long at Checkout

Please, tell me everything! It's always a pleasure when the cashier and bagger engage the customer. However, it's important to remember we're not at a social gathering—we're at the checkout.

I don't know how often I've stood at the conveyor watching the cashier and customer go on and on as if they were the only ones in the store.

I'm not talking about a 15-second chat, but ones that take several minutes.

This is especially prevalent in small towns. Where the cashier knows everyone and takes the time to find out how everyone is doing in the family, talk about what they did over the weekend, etc.

As I said, it's a nice thing and adds to the shopping experience. But...there's a limit to the amount of time that should be taken for this conversation.

Once you have your receipt and your groceries are safely in your cart, it's time to move on for the sake of customers behind you.

Going Back for Something

Wait here. I'll only be a second! You're standing at the conveyor, waiting patiently for your turn to check out, and the person in front of you suddenly realizes they forgot something.

They then take off looking for that forgotten item, thinking they'll only be a second, leaving their cart in the line and maybe even some of their items on the conveyor belt.

This can be awkward for everyone involved, as finding the item always takes longer than they think it will, and their turn at the checkout invariably comes while they're nowhere to be seen—thus holding up the entire checkout line.

These are the same people who would be complaining if they were in line and this happened to them.

Here's my advice. Instead of leaving everyone hanging, finish checking out, put your cart to the side, and then go back for that item. Or, you can ask the cashier to suspend your sale until you return.

It's the considerate thing to do.

Slow Checkout

Hey, some of us have places to go and people to see! How often have you been stuck in a slow line, moving like mud, when all you want to do is get on with your life? With today's scanning process and quick-to-load plastic bags, there isn't a legitimate reason for slow checkout.

Well, unless it's a new employee just learning the ropes. We've all been there. Or a cashier just wants to get through the day, and speed is of no concern to them.

I had a cashier recently who was really fast at scanning. It might have been the quickest I've ever seen. It gave me an idea for store managers: to have a monthly challenge for cashiers. Take six lanes and place thirty identical items on the belts in the same order. Then, race to see who can scan all thirty items the fastest and correctly. It would be fun for the employees and provide comic relief.

I think slow checkouts are (just one of the many reasons) why more stores are trending to self-checkout—which admittedly presents another level of slowness. (See "Self-Checkout.")

Parking Lot Behavior

Sure, park any way you like! I could talk about this all day, and I have. I hope you'll check out my first book in this series, *You're Driving Me Crazy!*, for even more on parking and parking lots.

Here we go. Let's shine a light on some of the all-too-common behaviors in and around the parking lot.

Many seem to feel a great need to park as close to the door as possible—so they can spend the next hour walking through the store. You turn down the parking aisle only to be delayed as the car in front of you waits for someone to pull out, just to get two spaces closer to the store.

Some drive an oversized vehicle and decide to park close to the store. This creates an interesting maze and blocks your view of pedestrians walking from the other side.

Most stores line the entrance with red or yellow stripes, clearly marking the space as reserved for delivery and emergency vehicles. While most people respect these rules, a few consider themselves above the law and ignore the restrictions, causing potential safety hazards.

Ever wonder why stores even bother painting parking lines? It seems like many folks don't bother to park within them.

Or they don't pull entirely into their spot. Are they distance-challenged? Or do they not care? Maybe a bit of both.

I've seen people take it upon themselves to teach such drivers a lesson by parking right up close to the vehicle in question, preventing the car's driver from getting in through the driver's side door. I disagree with this approach, as it runs the risk of retaliation, and patience is usually key in these situations.

Then there's the issue of vehicles waiting too closely for other drivers to load groceries into their cars, return their carts, and finally pull out. When that driver backs up, there's a car right behind them, causing unnecessary inconvenience and potential accidents.

And please, after loading your items in the car, don't sit there on your phone. Be aware of others who might be waiting to park in that space.

My advice? Just shake your head at all these behaviors and find a spot away from the chaos. Look for spots near cart returns or at the end of aisles, where there's less traffic and more space to maneuver, and lower risk of a ding.

Some prefer to park farther away, appreciating the exercise of walking across the parking lot and safely avoiding congestion. A few more steps won't hurt you. They're good for you!

I've found parking next to the cart return a game-changer. If it's a store I frequent, I aim for the same aisle and even the same spot if it's open. No more wandering around trying to remember where I parked. As I get older, this becomes more and more helpful.

(See also "Pedestrians in the Parking Lot.")

Shopping Carts

Thump, thump, thump. What's that noise? How often do you get halfway into the store and realize your cart is thumping?

I understand the carts take a lot of abuse and are wheeled across rough parking lot pavement every day, but the quality of the cart sets the tone for the shopping experience. Many times, there's something (like a rock) stuck on one of the wheels. If this is the case, a little trick to resolve this is to place your foot on the wheel in question (or each of them, if necessary) and allow the wheel to slide against your shoe. This will often remove the object in question.

But, back to the point. If the cart return employee finds a thumping cart, don't put it back for the next customer. Repair it or toss it.

Let's continue talking about carts, as they play a role in almost every shopping experience.

To paraphrase the famous *Field of Dreams* line, "If you build it, they'll come." That might apply to many things, but evidently not shopping cart corrals.

I'm sure you've seen stray shopping carts everywhere—on the sidewalk, on the curb, on the grass, against a light post, between cars, in front of vehicles, behind vehicles, and even on the street near the store.

The worst is an abandoned cart in a parking space. Not only does it block a car from parking, but it could also easily roll and slam into someone's vehicle after the culprit is long gone.

By returning your cart, you're not just preventing issues in the parking lot and keeping the carts in good condition, but also saving the store, and ultimately us, the money it would cost to pay store employees to round up stray carts.

It's always a good feeling to help others, and one simple way to do that is by offering to take someone's cart when they're finished with it. When I arrive at a store, I watch for people loading their cars to see if I might take their cart for them. They're generally delighted to have me save them the time to return it, as I am when someone offers to take my cart. These small acts of cooperation add to the pleasure of shopping.

And sometimes, you get into a store only to find no available carts. Another good reason to bring in a cart from the parking lot—to ensure you have one.

Restrooms

Clean Restrooms, clean store! Have you heard the old joke about the fellow who was late because he kept seeing signs along the road for "Clean Restrooms"—and cleaning all those restrooms took him a while?

We've all seen store bathrooms with issues like no toilet paper, no paper towels, trash can overflowing (if there is one), dirty toilets, dirty and wet floors, cobwebs, foul odor, crumpled paper towels on the counter, and on and on.

If you notice such any issues with the restroom, don't hesitate to bring it to the attention of the manager or customer service. Your feedback is valuable and can help improve the overall store experience.

A couple of ideas to make store bathrooms more customer-friendly include placing a trash receptacle near the door, allowing wipes and towels to be discarded upon leaving the room. And especially in women's restrooms, it's helpful to have a hook on the wall or door for hanging purses and coats. No one wants to put these items on the floor.

My advice is to check out the bathroom first when choosing a place to shop—clean bathroom, clean store.

And finally, it's always good to leave places, especially bathrooms, better than you found them.

Greetings!

Welcome to our store! Isn't it nice when, upon entering a store, you're greeted with a smile and a friendly "Welcome to our store"?

Most stores don't offer this courtesy, leaving me to feel I'm not important to them.

On the other hand, some stores have full-time greeters who create a welcoming environment and are also able to assist customers in finding particular items. This suggests to me these stores care about their customers and want them to have a positive shopping experience.

Full-time greeters not in your store's budget? That's okay. A simple smile will do.

Blocking the Aisle

Don't mind me! You spot them at the aisle's entrance, their cart or motorized vehicle creating an impenetrable barrier. It's as if they're in their own little world, oblivious to the traffic jam they're creating.

So, you stand there, grinning at the person (and the amused onlookers), as you attempt to navigate the shopping cart obstacle course. It's like a game, right?

Then, when you thought you had a clear path, another shopper appears from the opposite direction, sealing your fate.

If saying a polite "Excuse me" doesn't register with the person doing the blocking, I repeat it, louder. If this still doesn't work, I either move their cart for them or change directions and look for other items on my list, returning to that aisle later when there's less congestion.

(See also related topics like "Employees Not Giving the Customer the Right-of-Way" and "Motorized Carts Coming Through Regardless.")

Leaving and Entering an Aisle Without Looking

I think they taught us this in driving class. Here you are, peacefully pushing your cart along the central aisle, when suddenly, out of a side aisle, someone flies out cart first, without looking.

I've seen crashes with this move—both at the grocery store and on the road.

And then, adding insult to injury, some of the perpetrators of these crashes want you to move out of the way so they can continue.

I suggest conducting yourself like you're driving a car, nosing your cart to the end of the aisle, looking in both directions, and proceeding cautiously.

And remember when passing side aisles to leave plenty of room for others to make their unexpected appearances.

Simple, right?

Eating Unpaid Food While Shopping

Maybe I should bring a battery-powered microwave and cook some food while I'm shopping? You've probably heard the advice, "Never go shopping when you're hungry," but it's easy to forget—for me, too. I know it's hard to resist the temptation of all the delicious food in a grocery store, especially if our stomachs are growling.

But can we at least resist the urge to eat the food we want before paying for it? Let's wait until we've paid and left the store.

I recently saw a shopper meandering through the grocery store with a plastic tray of strawberries on the upper shelf of the cart. They were leaning on the cart handle as they slowly moved about the store, eating the strawberries.

Do you think when people shop for clothes, they try on something they're considering buying and then continue to shop in those clothes?

Eating food before paying can lead to misunderstandings with the store staff, and it's unfair to other shoppers who wait to pay for their items.

It's also a less-than-ideal example for impressionable children (yours or others) who might surmise from your behavior that eating food in the store is okay before paying. Or, worse, maybe they don't realize you plan to pay at all and think you're just helping yourself to the store's food, and they might do the same.

Instead of eating food that is not paid for, why not plan to eat at a designated area after you make your purchases?

At least wait until returning to your vehicle before diving into that potato salad!

Bumping People With the Cart

Excuse me? Did my feet just run into your cart? It seems that on every other trip to the store, someone is pushing their cart into me.

Probably just like their driving—they're not watching where they're going, or tailgating, and then, "bam!" These are probably the same people who are eager to get all their items on the belt in that small space behind yours, too (see "Placing Items on the Belt").

I've thought about wearing that sign on my back that says, "If you can read this, you're too close. Back off!"

As this book will emphasize in multiple places, paying attention to what's happening around us and respecting other shoppers' space is essential.

Not Putting Items Back Where They Came From

A package of bacon in the canned goods section? How often have you seen an item wildly out of place, obviously left there by someone who didn't want to be troubled to return it to where they got it? I see this more than I think I should, and it's costly to the store.

Let's not take that lazy route. If you decide not to purchase an item you've added to your cart, please return it to its original location. It only takes a couple of minutes, if that.

Children in the Store

It's called parenting! Aaaahh, kids in the grocery store. I loved going to the grocery store as a kid, and I think it's great for children to learn good shopping habits at a young age. And while I don't expect kids to always behave, I expect parents to parent.

Children running through the aisles, gathering as a group blocking the aisle, making a lot of noise, grabbing this and that and then leaving items strewn around. These are just some of the behaviors that drive me crazy.

It may take a village to raise a child, but that doesn't mean it's the job of store employees or other shoppers to mind your kids while you shop. They didn't sign on for that.

If you take your children to the store, please require that they behave. And if they don't, take them outside or away from others and calm them down. If that isn't possible, come back to the store another time. It's called parenting.

While I encourage everyone to follow these guidelines, I understand that there are times when, despite a parent's best efforts, a toddler can have a full-on meltdown during a necessary shopping trip. We may not always understand the specific challenges others are facing.

I found this great AI-generated description of good parenting on the Internet:

> Parenting in a grocery store can involve being prepared, setting expectations, and giving children a role. It's also important to be patient and remember that children are learning and exploring.

Prepare

- Make a list: Have children help write the list or choose a few items
- Pack a bag: Bring extra diapers, wipes, and a change of clothes

- Pick a time: Try shopping when children are well-rested and in a good mood

Set expectations

- Pick behaviors: Choose a few behaviors you want your child to engage in, like sitting in the cart or using their inside voice
- Offer a reward: Promise a treat if they meet certain expectations

Give children a role

- Let them help: Ask them to find items on the list or weigh produce
- Play a game: Turn shopping into a scavenger hunt or letter hunt
- Let them pick: Allow them to choose one new item from a specific section

Be patient

- Don't worry about time: Enjoy the moment and take breaks if needed
- Be realistic: Remember that children are learning by exploring
- Stay calm: Use gentle words to calm a child, and don't use physical punishment

(See also "Letting Little Kids Push the Cart.")

Employees Not Giving the Customer the Right-of-Way

Customer first, right? At most restaurants, you'll find employees stepping aside to allow customers to go by first. That's the way it should be.

This seems like one of those things a supervisor should teach grocery store employees.

I can't tell you the number of times an employee walks right in front of me without acknowledging me in any way as I'm perusing the shelves.

It's a sign of a good store when employees try to stay out of the way as much as possible, but—and this is important—they're still easy to find when a customer needs help (see also "An Employee Doesn't Offer Help").

These employees have their jobs because customers like to shop there. If workers ignore customers' need to navigate through the aisles or examine products near where employees are stocking, those frustrated customers might opt to shop elsewhere.

Some of these workers might be in a hurry collecting items for pickup orders, monopolizing the aisles with their huge carts, like janitor carts. It would be helpful for store management to make it clear to them that customers' access to the shelves should be the priority.

We're fortunate to have Publix here in Florida. Our local Publix management teams train the workers to be aware of their surroundings—to greet customers, ask if they need help, guide customers to the items they're looking for, and keep their stock carts out of the way.

To be sure, not all the people stocking shelves are store employees. Some are outside vendors with only one thing on their minds—get their products on the shelves so they can move on to the next store.

Some customers go to another aisle and wait to complete their shopping until the picker or stocker is finished, returning to that aisle later. I usually say something to the person to make them aware they're blocking the aisle. This can be done politely. Most will move their cart and make room.

Leaving Trash in the Cart

The cart isn't a trash can. If you're done shopping, dispose of any trash in a proper receptacle. It's easy.

What kind of trash might you find in a shopping cart? Well, an advertising flyer, used tissues, a completed shopping list, gum wrappers, food wrappers, sanitary wipes we use on the cart when entering the store.

Why would someone unload ten bags of groceries from the cart but leave their trash in the cart for someone else? We all share the responsibility for keeping our shopping environment clean and pleasant for everyone.

A well-run store should also ensure carts are cleaned of trash between uses. This is another indication (like restrooms) of cleanliness and customer care.

If you do find someone else's trash in your cart, go ahead and throw it away. One exception—if the trash left in the cart is a used wipe, leave it. It's probably loaded with germs.

And, concerning germs, it's a good habit to keep hand sanitizer in the car to clean your hands after each shopping stop. Many began doing this during the COVID-19 pandemic and have continued.

Bottom line: always remember to throw your trash away. It's the right thing to do, like returning the cart and parking between the lines.

Getting in Front of You While You're Browsing Products

Am I invisible? If I had that superpower, I'd be doing something more exciting than grocery shopping. Have you ever had someone suddenly block your view while you're browsing products?

Let's give them the benefit of the doubt. Likely, they're not trying to be rude. Maybe, like other examples of oblivious behavior in this book, they're just not paying attention to what's happening around them. It's another reminder for all of us to stay aware of our surroundings.

If they're too lost in la-la land to catch themselves and move out of the way, a polite "Excuse me" should work. If not, I've been known to tap them on the shoulder to let them know I'm there.

This has elicited mixed reactions, including looking blankly at me but continuing to stand there. Most of the time, I get a simple apology and they move out of my way.

But in particularly hopeless cases, I move on and return to that section later.

Pedestrians in the Parking Lot

Stop, Look, and Listen. Let's do some math. An average person weighs 150 pounds (just a guess), and the average car weighs 4,000 pounds (again, just a guess). If you take a 4,000-pound vehicle and throw it against a 150-pound person, which do you think will suffer the most damage? Exactly.

So why do people walk straight out of the store and cross the road to the parking lot without looking? It's as if the classic "Stop, Look, and Listen" rule has been forgotten. Let's bring it back to the forefront of our pedestrian safety practices.

This was one of my, well, "driving" forces for writing *You're Driving Me Crazy!*—as a reminder to be aware of what's going on around us at all times so we can act accordingly and prevent unwanted situations.

Here are a couple more ways to be safer as a pedestrian in parking lots:

- Walk facing traffic instead of with your back to traffic. It's the same as walking along a road. Parents should teach their children this from an early age so it becomes second nature, but clearly (based on walkers I see with their backs to traffic) that doesn't always happen.

- Remember you're harder for drivers to see if you wear dark clothes at night. If you have a choice, wear lighter, brighter clothes.
- When you're the one driving in a parking lot—or anywhere else—especially be on the lookout for pedestrians wearing dark colors at night and/or walking with their backs to traffic. Your carefulness can prevent a tragic, even fatal, accident.

But please, pedestrians, don't leave it up to drivers to see you. They should, but they might be distracted by other cars and people in the parking lot. You know about defensive driving; that's the mindset you should have as a pedestrian, too.

Remember, you're the first line of defense for your safety while walking in the parking lot. Take responsibility and stay alert.

(See also "Drivers Not Stopping for Pedestrians at Entrance" and "Backing Up in the Parking Lot Without Looking.")

Loitering

I'm just hanging out. Do they have nothing going on in their lives, no place to hang out except a grocery store? Worse, are they "casing the joint," looking for an opportunity to shoplift?

Or maybe hoping to find a romantic partner by hanging around the produce section, striking up conversations about artichokes?

If loiterers aren't causing any harm, perhaps they're just enjoying a leisurely stroll through the aisles. It may be unusual, but it's not necessarily a cause for concern. After all, we all have our own ways of spending time.

These loiterers may be just like me, passionate about grocery shopping. They might be enjoying the variety of products, seeking inspiration for their next meal, or simply appreciating the ambiance of the store.

Approaching other shoppers for money or behaving in a threatening manner isn't acceptable, however. If you notice a loiterer making others uncomfortable, alerting store management is the responsible thing to do.

Dealing with Deli Line-Cutters

Hey, is someone cutting the cheese, er, line? There you are, your mouth watering at the thought of that delicious sub you're about to order, when suddenly, out of nowhere, someone walks right up to the counter and orders ahead of you. It's frustrating, isn't it?

To give them the benefit of the doubt, when you approach a busy deli, it's often hard to recognize any order or line. So those who butt in line might only be doing so out of confusion and might be grateful to learn where the line is. I usually speak up and point it out to them.

But it really comes down to the person behind the counter to set the record straight.

The best solution is simple—a numbered ticket system. With this system, you pull a number and patiently wait for it to be called, ensuring everyone gets their turn and no one gets overlooked. (See also "Cutting in Line at the Cash Register.")

Littering

Excuse me, did you drop these two twenty-dollar bills? I can't wrap my head around deliberate littering, especially in stores—who even does that? What kind of statement are they trying to make, "I'm a self-hating slob"?

Stores, including the ones you frequent, have made it incredibly convenient for you to dispose of your trash. They've strategically placed multiple containers by the entrance and elsewhere.

Of course, we're all human and sometimes things slip out of our hands, pockets, or wallets. It's a gentle reminder to properly stow your money, ensuring you aren't leaving a trail of your hard-earned bills fluttering behind you as you leave the store!

I hope you'll check out my more extensive section on littering in my first book of this series, *You're Driving Me Crazy!*, an entertaining and practical guide for becoming an even finer driver than I know you already are.

Also, see the "Leaving Trash in the Cart" section in this book.

Using an Express Lane With Too Many Items

Do you ever wonder if they even bother to count the items in their cart? They get their stuff on the belt and say, "Oh, I just realized I have too many items." Would the cashier force them to return everything in their cart and go to another lane? It seems like they're betting not.

It would be fun to follow these people to their vehicle because they've likely parked their Suburban in a "compact only" spot. Or, worse yet, in the handicapped spot with no handicap (other than being inconsiderate). Then, as they drive off, watch as they knowingly exceed the speed limit but act surprised when a police officer pulls them over.

There have been times I've been in a situation where the 20-or-less lane is empty, and the cashier called me over. I'd decline, saying I'd wait, but they insisted because no one was there. It seems like every time, without fail, as soon as I placed my items on the belt, customers with a handful of things would show up and give me "the look."

After numerous such frustrating experiences, I've decided I'll no longer use the express lane for more than eight items. Why eight? It's just a number I know will work—with room to spare.

Touching Fresh Bakery Items

Those rolls are not for juggling! It's too common to see people handling unwrapped bread, rolls, and other baked goods. This is a practice that needs to change for the sake of public health.

Even if you have clean hands (and I doubt that's the case after collecting other items throughout the store), you shouldn't touch unwrapped bakery items. Unlike fruits and vegetables, bakery items can't be washed. Touching them can transfer bacteria and other harmful pathogens, increasing the risk of foodborne illnesses.

While it's tempting to test the freshness of bakery items, it's important to remember that if you touch them, you should go ahead and buy them.

If you have a concern that something has been handled, simply ask the clerk in the bakery section to get you a fresh item.

Rudeness to Employees

Service workers aren't punching bags. By now, you've probably surmised, rightfully, that I'd sympathize with just about any shopping grievance you could have.

But this is the most important message of the entire book. *Be kind to people, please.*

Some people look down on service workers. It's a shame because they add much to our quality of life and deserve our appreciation. And they're just like you, doing a job.

No matter your complaint, please don't go off on store employees, even if you're sure it's all their fault. It's a terrible habit to get into.

The satisfaction of unleashing a tirade is short-lived, and you rarely get the desired result—unless your goal is to earn a spot among that store's least-favorite customers, should you ever want to shop there again.

This also applies to service workers on the phone and online. Though we aren't face to face with them, they're still human beings with feelings.

Let's try not to be the reason an employee has a bad day or grows to hate their job.

If you have a beef, seek out the manager and respectfully—and I do mean respectfully—explain the problem.

I repeat, because this is important: if you have a concern, remember you have the power to address it respectfully and constructively. Seek out the manager and calmly tell your side of the story.

Sometimes, it's simply a misunderstanding, which may be yours (or mine).

Being Loud

Pipe down! Some people are just naturally loud. You've been around them.

Go to a restaurant or a bar, and you can always hear that one person louder than everyone else. They become the unwelcome soundtrack of the evening as others are forced to listen to their conversation willy-nilly.

One encounters them in stores, too, shouting to someone a few feet away. It's jarring. Maybe there's a reason for it; for instance, they've gotten used to talking loudly to a partner who's hard of hearing. I sympathize.

But if we can, let's try to use our indoor voice in public places. Be quiet! Let me think!

I believe grocery shopping is ideally a quiet time for thinking and reflection. People are busy making decisions, reading labels, calculating costs, and planning meals. If I could have my way, grocery stores would have the same rules as libraries.

Cutting in Line at the Cash Register

Mind if I cut in? For some, a line is nothing more than a suggestion—for others.

I suspect these are the same people who park by the front door, occupy a handicapped space (and they're not handicapped—except for their personality), and generally put themselves ahead of everyone else.

I sometimes say something to them and respond accordingly to their reaction. The older I get, the bolder I am about confronting behavior like this. (See also "Dealing with Deli Line-Cutters.")

However, at the end of the day, it's one person and maybe ten minutes of my time. We all have to consider the costs of our actions. Is it worth it to cause a scene and get labeled as "that person"?

I sympathize—the line is long, and you hate standing in line. That's true for many of us. Or perhaps the cashier is your cousin or your buddy—shouldn't that earn you the special privilege of slipping in front? No.

Please don't do it. Other people's time is just as valuable as our own. If a line seems unbearably long and you only have a few items, you can consider whether you'd rather return them to their proper shelves and leave. Try a different store, or come back later.

On Saying "Thank You"

Tausendmal vielen Dank (Thank you a thousand times). The "thank you" elevates both the giver and the receiver. It's a win-win, in shopping and in general, in little and big ways.

Say "thank you" to the cashier and person who bags your items.

And don't stop there; thank the person who helps you in the store, at the deli, as well as the butcher, pastry people, pharmacy, customer service desk, those who let you go in front of them in line, hold the door open for you, and even the employee who returns your cart for you. Especially thank people who fulfill your requests.

Being generous with thanks to others for their help and kind gestures is an excellent habit to get into, and (for anyone who needs to hear this) it's not too late to start right now. Beyond shopping, I promise this will lead—you might be surprised how quickly—to happier relationships, more enjoyable opportunities, and a better quality of life.

Abandoning a Cart

Remember the Golden Rule? We've talked about leaving carts in the parking lot, but what about the ones inside the store?

A shopper decides they don't need a cart during their visit and leaves it in the aisle, forcing others to maneuver around the empty cart. This can make it difficult with oncoming shoppers and/or narrow aisles.

Or maybe it's not abandoned—perhaps the customer left the cart momentarily to find an item. When they temporarily parked it, there were no other shoppers nearby. But then someone invariably comes along, needing to get to the exact shelves the cart is blocking.

The Golden Rule—treating others how we'd like to be treated—is an unbeatable guide for our shopping behavior and most other life situations. It reminds us to think of and be considerate of others—other shoppers, store employees.

As responsible shoppers, it's our duty to return an unwanted cart to where we got it, or if we leave our cart alone for a minute—say, to slip into a crowded aisle to pick up two things—we're careful to park it in an out-of-the-way spot. The out-of-the-way part is important, making an effort to find a place that is truly out of the way.

I must admit, sometimes I go into a store to get one or two things and soon find myself with more than I can carry. Maybe that happens to you, too. This is the one exception, when I'm happy to see an abandoned cart.

People Who Shop Behind You

Back off, Jack…! Do you ever feel like you're being stalked while shopping? What is it with people who stay right behind you throughout the store?

Some will pass you only to get right in front of you. And then, soon after you pass them, they pass you again. (Have you ever had drivers do this to you on the road? That's what it reminds me of.)

Are we shopping for exactly the same things? Do they need to see what I'm getting to determine what they want? Is it my magnetic personality?

As much as I'd like to make a new friend, please give me my space while shopping.

If they don't back off, I admit I've been known to intentionally slow down, forcing them to pass me or at least giving them a taste of similar frustration to what they've caused me.

Expired Items

Yuck, this milk is sour! I'll bet most people don't look at expiration dates on their food products. But let me suggest you do. Some stores may not be as vigilant, and you could find yourself buying something expired or about to expire. By checking expiration dates, you can avoid buying something past its prime.

Usually, the older products are placed at the front, with the newer ones in the back. This is most common with dairy items such as milk.

If you come across an expired product—or find you've taken home a spoiled product—please alert the manager for two important reasons:

firstly, so they can investigate why that item was on the shelf; and secondly, to prevent someone else from buying the item, or others like it.

If the store is so seedy the management doesn't seem to care that your milk was sour, they probably won't be in business much longer. Other customers have likely had similar experiences, and at least you tried.

Opening a New Checkout Lane

I thought they said, "NEXT in line"! You're patiently standing in a long line with only one or two registers open. But then a cashier opens a new lane and says, "I'll take the next one in line."

Then, people rush to the new lane from the back of the lines. Or it's someone stalking an empty lane in hopes one will open.

> "Anyone who believes the competitive spirit in America is dead has never been in a supermarket when the cashier opens another check-out line." ~ Ann Landers

Maybe I'm hard of hearing (which I am), but I thought they said "next in line."

Kudos to the cashiers who, when opening a new lane, come over to the person waiting next in line at another lane and guide them to their register. This helps eliminate that mad rush by others.

Yes, we're all in a hurry, but others' time is just as important as our own. Letting the people there before us go first is not just a matter of courtesy; it's a matter of fairness.

(See also "Not Enough Checkout Lanes Open.")

Handing the Cashier Trash to Throw Away

I'm sure you have a trash can back there somewhere, right? Maybe you've seen this—shoppers who have finished a bag of chips or something while browsing and then hand the empty bag to the cashier for disposal.

I think that's inappropriate and causes inconvenience to the cashier—but then, to that customer's credit, at least they aren't littering or leaving it in the cart.

It's still a better habit to take responsibility for our trash and dispose of it ourselves in the designated bins.

All About the Phone (and Speakerphone)

They must be on the phone with someone famous, and want to make sure all the strangers in the store know it!

While I understand the necessity of being on your phone, such as discussing a purchase with your spouse or handling an urgent call from your kids, why do some individuals feel the need to broadcast their conversations at a volume that permeates the entire store? Don't they even have respect for their own privacy?

As I've mentioned before, in my opinion the shopping experience should be akin to a visit to the library. It's a time for quiet contemplation, a chance to think and plan without unnecessary distractions. Those loud, blaring voices shatter the peace.

It's a simple choice—either talk at a reasonable volume or find a more suitable place to continue your conversation.

And then some are so focused on their phone they have no idea what's happening around them. For instance, I was in the store recently and had to ask three times for three young people to move over so I could get by. Their cart was blocking the aisle, and all three stood there looking at their phones, oblivious to their surroundings.

Lastly, while I understand the temptation to hand a phone to a restless child, the shopping experience is a valuable opportunity for parents to model considerate behavior. By setting a good example early, you can prevent them from becoming the loud, aisle-blocking shoppers of the future.

See also "Talking on the Phone While Going Through the Checkout."

Employees Rude/Unhelpful to Customers

Customers are the whole reason you have your job! On the flip side of customers being rude to employees, we have employees being rude to customers. It's upsetting to see an employee arguing with or insulting a customer, or sullenly ignoring a customer who wants help (see also "An Employee Doesn't Offer Help").

Maintaining a professional demeanor is crucial, regardless of the customer's behavior. This doesn't mean giving in to bullying or granting unreasonable requests. Still, the employee must keep calm and seek a solution to benefit the customer, calling in a manager if need be—Customer Service 101.

If an employee is rude, you can find a manager and explain the situation. If the manager is unwilling to work with you, you have every reason to leave the store and shop elsewhere.

But I'm guessing the manager wants to know so they can resolve the issue and keep you as a customer. The employee may already have a record of being rude, and this might be the time to justify letting that person go.

Coupons Are Great, But…

What do you mean, this coupon expired two years ago? Won't you take it anyway? Oh yes. Coupons used to be a way of life. It's a great way to get people to shop at your store.

When I was growing up, with each purchase we earned S&H Green Stamps (remember those?), which we'd accumulate to exchange for products.

It's great that stores offer coupons as they can save a lot of money, a boon for those on a limited budget.

However, the use and presentation of coupons can be an issue.

For instance, when the customer presents expired coupons and argues with the cashier they should be accepted anyway. (See also "Unsolvable Mysteries at the Checkout.")

And it's always fun to be behind someone with a gazillion coupons, and the cashier has to scan each of them.

> **Did You know:** Couponing is an effective strategy for cutting grocery costs, and the majority of shoppers seem to be using them. Women are more likely to clip coupons, with 57% of female shoppers collecting them compared to 41% of men. (Source: https://www.creditdonkey.com/grocery-shopping-statistics.html)

Nowadays, our local store (along with others) has a membership system that simplifies the couponing process. No more fumbling with paper coupons—the discounts you might see in a flyer or around the store automatically apply when an item is scanned. It's a time-and-money saver we can all appreciate.

If you do use paper coupons, have them ready and present them to the cashier at the beginning of your checkout.

Not Knowing How to Use the Credit Card Swipe

I don't know how much easier this can be. Have you ever found yourself behind a low-tech person at the register who seems to be navigating the credit card process for the first time? They fumble with the card, unsure of the right way to swipe, insert, or tap. Credit/debit cards are so standard that witnessing someone struggle with this can be surprising. And, we might think, it's just our luck to be behind them at that moment.

But, for whatever reason, as incredible as it might seem to a card-swiping pro like yourself, maybe it is their first time using it. It's important to remember everyone has their own unique circumstances. They could be older and have always used cash or checks. They might have finally joined the twenty-first century by getting their first debit card, like my editor confesses she did just last year. Or maybe their usual shopper, their spouse, is in the hospital recovering from surgery. We can't always know what's going on in someone else's life, but we can always offer kindness.

When I see someone struggling with the card scanner, I offer help if they seem open to that. Patience and understanding go a long way in these situations. You might make someone's day—and, in doing so, also your own.

If you're unfamiliar with this technology and need to learn, try to go when the store isn't crowded to a checkout lane that isn't busy. Then a friend or family member, or a friendly cashier, can teach you in an unhurried way.

The good news is, as I said, it's easy. If this technology is new to you, don't worry, and don't be embarrassed. You'll be swiping your card with confidence in no time.

Freezer Doors

Do you prefer your ice cream melted? It's helpful when people look at the freezer items through the glass door, decide what they want, and then open the door and get the item. When they hold the freezer door open while selecting, the glass gets all fogged up—so the next customer can't view the items through the door and has to hold the door open while choosing items—and so on.

As I've mentioned before, I have a low level of OCD, if you haven't already noticed by reading this far. I'm constantly arranging packages on the shelves so the labels are out, picking up fallen items, and even returning items moved by other customers to the wrong place.

Some freezers are supposed to close automatically, but some will get close but not completely shut. I think it's just a courtesy thing to shut the door when you finish, or if you see one open.

Don't worry, even though the person before me didn't shut the freezer door, I'll get it!

Throwing Crumpled Bills on the Counter

Here you go! I hope that covers it. I see this often, especially in convenience stores.

The customer is paying in cash, and as they pull their money from their jeans pocket (one crumpled bill at a time), they toss it on the counter.

Imagine being the cashier. You must pick up the folded or crumpled bills and then straighten, organize, and count them.

If you use cash, have your bills straightened, facing in the same direction, and sorted by denomination. Then, hand the appropriate amount to the cashier.

Also, you might find using a billfold or wallet a nice improvement over the habit of cramming bills in your pocket. As an adult, you deserve to afford yourself that dignity, and you'll be helping the hardworking cashier at the same time.

Talking on the Phone While Going Through the Checkout

Rude! Now, this really gets under my skin. It's one thing to be strolling through the store on your phone, speaking softly and staying out of the way. But when a customer is on the phone during checkout, I think it shows a lack of respect, consideration, and courtesy to the cashier.

What kind of conversation needs to happen at that moment? If it's an emergency, that's another story. But to simply be talking to a friend when you're supposed to engage the cashier?

I doubt people who do this mean to be rude, but it's still rude.

Please, let's make an effort not to talk on the phone while going through the regular checkout with a cashier. If it's the self-checkout, I'll cut you some slack if you keep scanning and paying.

Dressing in Pajamas

It's a pajama party! Well, times have certainly changed. Maybe it's just me, but we used to clean up and get into some nice clothes before we went out in public. Not anymore. Do you miss those days? Me, too.

I'm constantly amazed by the things people wear out in public. And I see so many people wearing pajamas. Especially college students.

It should go without saying, though, that just because we disagree with another shopper's fashion choices doesn't mean we should point that out to them. That takes inappropriateness to another level. Instead, let's be kind and polite and chalk it all up to human variety.

Maybe every generation goes through some version of dressing in ways that appall their elders. And they end up turning out all right, after all.

But you can rarely go wrong by dressing to respect the people who'll have to look at you. Go by that rule, and it will make dressing easy for the rest of your life.

Licking Fingers to Sort Bills at the Checkout

Nobody wants to see that. It's unpleasant to see people licking their fingers to sort their dollar bills and then handing them to the cashier. This seemingly harmless, too-common habit can spread germs and pose a health risk—to others and the licker.

If it's a struggle to separate your bills, take your time; we'd rather wait.

Enough germs are being transferred throughout the store as products are being handled by people who have touched other things, without having to contend with someone's actual saliva.

Let's give some consideration to others' health and our own. Please refrain from licking your fingers. If you've gotten into that habit, it's a good habit to get out of.

Spilled Items Left on the Floor

"Pick up on aisle four!" I'm surprised there aren't more spills in a grocery store. Maybe there are, and I'm just not there to see it each time.

Occasionally, something like a jar of pickles is dropped; everyone looks surprised and at each other ("It wasn't me!"). Then, "Pick up on aisle four!"

Seeing the spillage and realizing it's been there for a while isn't a good sign.

While it's true customers should alert an employee when a spill occurs, it's equally important that store workers are vigilant, scanning aisles for potential hazards. After all, customer safety should be their top priority.

An Employee Doesn't Offer Help

Maybe they don't want to be annoying? I realize some customers prefer to be given space and not approached with, "Is there anything I can help you with?" And that some store employees try to be sensitive to that and not come across as overly aggressive. With this in mind, I try to give the benefit of the doubt to employees who don't offer help.

But I've been in stores where I've spent a while trying to find a product. Right next to me was an employee stocking shelves. They wouldn't bother even to look over, let alone notice I was having trouble finding the item I was looking for. So I'd ask them for help—and often, it felt like I was interrupting them from their work.

It would have been nice if they'd at least said hi, nodded, or even shot me a friendly look, indicating they were *open* to helping.

I know this is a generalization, as many do make customer service their priority, as it should be. They consider it part of their job, and I appreciate and prefer employees looking out for me. I experience it as kindness, and I thank them for it. (See also my shout-out to Publix for their exemplary customer service under "Employees Not Giving the Customer the Right-of-Way.")

Drivers Not Stopping for Pedestrians at Entrance

Coming through! Only foot traffic (including the occasional motorized cart) is going in and out of the store, so drivers should know shoppers will come out at any moment to cross to the parking lot.

Always be on the lookout for pedestrians at the entrance/exit of the store. Your vigilance will prevent accidents.

Stop and pedestrian signs are placed for guidance, and it's our responsibility as drivers to obey them. And to keep our speed down.

(See also "Pedestrians in the Parking Lot.")

Personal Cleanliness

Pee-Yew! Of course, I get that many of us must stop at the store after work or have other situations that don't comfortably allow for freshly showering and changing clothes right before stopping at the store.

> People often say that motivation doesn't last. Well, neither does bathing—that's why we recommend it daily. —Zig Ziglar

But a reasonably recent shower, clean-ish clothes, and good deodorant, if you can manage those things, are respectful to our fellow shoppers and ourselves, contributing to a more pleasant public space.

Trash on the Floors

Is this the dump? Keeping the store clean should be a task for all employees.

> "Cleanliness is next to Godliness." --John Wesley, 1791 sermon, "On Dress."

As you might suspect by now, if I see trash on the floor of a store, I'll often pick it up myself. Of course, it depends on what that trash is.

I especially look out for items someone could slip or trip on—a flat piece of cardboard, a clothes hanger, a child's ball.

I believe a clean store is a good store. A dirty store is one to avoid. If cleaning isn't being done, I figure the more important tasks may also be ignored, and it might be best to go elsewhere if you prefer fresh eggs and milk that didn't expire a month ago.

(See also "Littering," "Restrooms," and "Expired Items.")

Rotten Fruit and Vegetables

Isn't this just a little…overripe? Our local stores do a great job of staffing the fresh produce aisles. They work hard to keep the produce stocked and appropriately displayed and make sure spoiled produce has been removed.

Produce is one of those areas that needs constant attention. So many people pick through items and then return them to another spot on the shelf. Bags of potatoes are taken from the front row, leaving the remaining ones sitting high up and out of reach.

I recommend checking out the produce section first to get an idea of the store's attention to detail. If you find spoiled produce, I'm guessing the bathrooms aren't clean either, and there's litter on the floors.

A shout out to my favorite fruit and vegetable market, The Bushel Stop in Zephyrhills, Florida, which has an amazing selection of local produce. My good friends, Maria and her husband, own the store and work hard every day to ensure all the produce is clean, fresh, and displayed neatly. I always know I'll get the best.

Stop by The Bushel Stop and be sure to tell them I sent you. You can thank me later.

No Gridlock at the Checkout, Please!

May I get through? I understand the spaces around the checkout lanes are sometimes limited due to displays and close proximity to the aisles. When you're in a long checkout line, however, it's a sign of respect to be mindful not to block the "roadway" for others still shopping.

It's like being careful in a traffic jam not to let yourself get stuck blocking a crossroad when their light turns green. (This is usually a lesson a driver only has to learn once: block a crossroad, and a cacophony of horn-blowing and angry shouts is generally forthcoming.)

Some of these aisle-blocking shoppers look at you blankly, then look straight ahead as if to say, "I'm not moving; go around." If you say, "Excuse me," they hesitate to move, fearing someone taking their space.

They spent the last hour wandering through the store, but now they feel like they can't allow anything to slow down their speedy exit!

If you are in a long line at the checkout, try to create a curved line so as to keep the aisles open for others who are still shopping.

Handing Items to the Cashier

Thanks, but the cashier has it under control. I know you're just trying to help, but do the cashier a favor and put your items on the belt. The cashiers I've talked to don't need you to hand them your items one by one.

I don't see this happen often, but when I do, either the cashier will say something to the customer or grimace and continue checking out.

The cashiers have a well-practiced routine as they scan items from the belt, and it is best to let them do their thing.

Motorized Carts Coming Through Regardless (and Blocking the Aisles)

"Beep, beep!" My dad struggled to walk through the grocery store in his final years. We decided it might be a good idea to try a motorized cart.

My dad, bless his heart, was running into shelves, people, and anything else in his way. That was the first and last time we did that!

I understand it has to be difficult to maneuver that vehicle through narrow aisles filled with people and carts, so I cut them slack. If a motorized cart is blocking an aisle, I'm rarely in such a hurry that I can't return a few minutes later when the aisle is clear.

Even better, we can go up to them and ask if they need any help getting something off the shelf.

Backing Up in the Parking Lot Without Looking

Let's play Frogger! Always be on the lookout for those people who get in their car and immediately back out without looking—or not looking carefully enough. This lack of attention not only increases the potential for hitting a passing car, but also poses a serious threat to people walking behind vehicles who aren't always easily seen.

So stay alert for people entering their vehicles and the telltale reverse lights. Your vigilance can prevent accidents.

As a driver, remember that there's not always a clear view behind you, especially when a bulky truck or van is parked nearby.

And, as suggested earlier in the book, if your plans might include walking in a parking lot (or anywhere there's traffic) after dark, remember that wearing dark clothes at night can decrease your visibility to drivers—so it's not a bad idea to wear lighter, brighter clothes if you have that choice. (See also "Pedestrians in the Parking Lot.")

Driving Down the Wrong Direction in the Parking Lot

The parking lot isn't a free-for-all! We follow the direction of traffic on the road, right, so why can't people manage that in the parking lot? It's straightforward. Directional arrows are there to guide you, painted on the road, or all cars parked on each side face the same direction at an angle. It's a simple system anyone can follow.

I've been in situations where a car is approaching me from the wrong direction in the parking lot. They may not know they're going the wrong way (although I believe most of them do as the direction of the lane is clearly marked) and wait for me to do something. There are no available slots to turn into, so we sit there and look at each other awkwardly. I have to get out and politely explain to them they're going the wrong way. They have to back up. By then, there's another car behind my car. Yes, this has happened.

Please make sure you're going in the right direction when entering the parking lanes.

Not Enough Checkout Lanes Open

Is there a manager working today? Once you're done shopping, you want to pay for your items and get home. But too many times, I've found myself standing in a long line while several checkout lanes are without cashiers.

Look at the others in line; they're thinking (and maybe saying) the same thing you are—open more lanes, people!

This situation could be easily avoided with better supervision and anticipation of customer traffic. There should be a manager on the floor, or even one of the cashiers, who will watch the store's occupancy and anticipate the number of shoppers nearing the end of their shopping.

I know checkouts come in waves, but please have cashiers ready. They can do something else while waiting for customers: straightening magazines, putting candy in order, or cleaning the belt. Something.

More stores are now incorporating self-checkout stations. I think it's a good idea. In some cases, scanners are a part of the cart, and you scan items as you place them in the cart. Click pay on the cart and head home. Problem solved.

(See also "Opening a New Checkout Lane.")

Stealing Slots in the Parking Lot

What the &%@#?! Have you ever found yourself in a potential parking lot showdown at the grocery store? You're not alone. This situation has sparked many a heated exchange.

You're waiting patiently for a car to back out of its space, ready to pull in. Then just as that vehicle passes you, someone from the other direction swoops in and takes your spot.

Giving them the benefit of the doubt, they may very well not even notice you and think they're simply pulling into a space, so if you confront them, they'll have no idea what you're talking about.

I might have engaged in a verbal sparring match with the other driver back in the day if I suspected it wasn't just an innocent mistake. But now, I ask myself, "Do I really need to make this situation worse?" (Note: this is a good thing to ask ourselves in all kinds of life situations.)

So, these days, I choose to drive on by and find another spot. I might release some tension with a few choice words only I can hear, but I don't let it ruin my day.

Leave Heavy Items in the Cart

You can save weightlifting for the gym (and save your back). I see customers struggle to lift heavy items, such as large bags of dog food or cases of bottled water, from the cart to the belt. Then, the cashier has to lug the item through the scanner and slide it down to the bagging area.

It is best to leave these items in the cart and let the cashier punch in the code or scan them with their hand scanner.

This system is also convenient for semi-heavy multiple, identical items like gallon jugs. You can hand one of them to the cashier to scan and show her the eight others in the cart.

Adopting this practice will benefit everyone—it's easier on your back and the cashier's, too.

Reaching Over You to Grab Something

Uh, we'll dance later, okay? I was in the store the other day reading labels on some canned foods when suddenly, I felt a bump on my shoulder. I looked around, and someone was reaching over me to grab something off the shelf. No "excuse me," no apology, just acting like casually bumping into another person is a normal part of shopping.

This is a reminder of the importance of respecting other shoppers' personal space. My friends and family will tell you I'm a people person—heck, I'd even give you a big hug. But I'd still rather not be crowded or jostled while shopping.

Is it that hard to wait until the other customer is done at that spot and moves on? It usually won't be long. Or, at least, have the courtesy to say "excuse me" if, for some reason, you're in a terrible rush and *must* reach past another shopper to get those peaches within the next few seconds.

Placing a Basket Full of Items on the Belt

Newbie shopper? Occasionally, someone places their handbasket, full of items, on the belt. This is a no-no. It's inconvenient for the cashier to unload all the items and deal with your basket. Then, the items might be sent on to the bagging area in non-ideal order.

If you have a basket of items, take them out and place them on the belt in the proper order (see "Placing Items on the Belt"—it's easy) to ensure a smooth checkout process, and then return the basket to one of the basket receptacles on your way out of the store.

Taking Multiple Free Samples and Hanging Out at That Spot

If you're that hungry, I'll buy you lunch! This is common at Costco, where several free sample stations are scattered throughout the store.

It's frustrating to come around the corner only to find a half dozen people standing around eating the samples while their carts are blocking the aisles. These people drive me crazy! And Costco has wide aisles!

If you're going to get a sample, find an out-of-the-way spot for your cart, walk over to the sample station, get your sample, say "Thank you," and return to your cart.

For folks actually hoping to make a meal out of free samples, it might be worth investigating more effective, satisfactory ways of getting fed.

Unruly Pets

I love dogs. Most people do. But . . . I understand the joy of bringing our furry friends along to the store. But if you have a dog or pet not trained to be friendly, quiet, and passive in the store, please don't take them. (This applies to children as well!)

It's essential to consider the safety and comfort of other shoppers before bringing your pet along. This responsibility falls on us as pet owners. Remember that people, including children, might want to stop and pet the animal. Pets should never bark or snap at other shoppers.

I do enjoy seeing service dogs in the store. They're always so well-behaved, more so than some shoppers.

I once stopped to ask a woman about her service dog. She told me the dog just got out of prison. What? Prison? A dog? I was stunned and asked what crime the dog had committed. She said the dog was working with inmates, helping them learn to be around dogs, fostering responsibility, empathy, and valuable life skills. That was cool!

Crowding You at Checkout

Give me some breathing room, please! There you are, putting your card in the card reader as the cashier scans your items, and the person behind you is edging uncomfortably close as if to say, "Hurry up, I'm next!"

A recurring theme in this book is respect for others' personal space while shopping. But why do some people need to invade that space at the checkout? It's not just intrusive; it can be downright intimidating.

I've been known to stare at them, say "Seriously?" and ask them politely to back off a little. But since they've managed to squeeze themselves between their cart and me with no room to move, there's not much you can do but keep going to the end of the lane and get out of their way.

Remember, crowding the person in front of us won't make the checkout process any faster. So, let's practice a little patience and relax for a minute. Our turn is coming right up.

Parking in Handicapped Spaces Without a Sticker

Blind driver? As a community of drivers, we all share the responsibility of respecting handicapped spaces. No doubt like many of you, I'm always on the lookout for handicap tags on cars parked in these spaces.

Remember, though, as a close friend of mine once told me, "Not all handicaps are visual." For instance, some people struggle to breathe, making a long walk from the parking lot a daunting task. So we should avoid judging if someone who looks non-disabled gets out of the vehicle.

This is something that hits home for me. I actually have a handicap tag, but I use it sparingly, only taking the handicapped spot if necessary.

And it's a clear misuse of handicapped spaces when someone uses their disability as an excuse to park across two or three spots to protect their fancy car.

Disregard for Older and Disabled People

Be kind, please. Older and disabled individuals are navigating through what can be a challenging task for them. They may not move as swiftly as others, but patience and kindness can go a long way. Let's extend some understanding as they go about their shopping.

Why not stop and ask them if they need help? Many times, they do. They may need help reaching or finding an item or lifting something too heavy for them off the shelf.

This is also true when walking to your car and seeing someone needing help loading their vehicle. (A caveat here: please don't hold it against them if they refuse help—it might be a matter of pride or mistrusting strangers. But you can still offer in good faith.)

Next time you're in the store, take a moment to assist someone if they seem to need it. Your help matters. And you might find the rest of your day is a little happier, too—funny how that works.

Drunk Shoppers

Breathalyzer on aisle five! Have you ever seen someone drunk at the store? Yeah? I said, "seen," not "been"!

I've seen people mildly inebriated to full-on drunk. Occasionally, you'll see a drunk shopper bothering people and creating an uncomfortable scene. They might be loud, disruptive, or aggressive toward other customers or staff.

At the very least, I suggest you find another aisle quickly. If you think it's called for, seek out the manager for assistance before the situation escalates.

Interestingly, some stores have an area where you can drink beer and wine. I suppose this is an attraction and may even result in more customer purchases. A note here that in many states, it's illegal to sell alcohol to someone visibly drunk.

While I enjoy a good beer as much as the next person, I advise against mixing alcohol with shopping. Alcohol can cloud your judgment, leading to actions you'd usually avoid, such as making unwise purchases.

This goes for store employees, too—two gins and tonics before work will lead to mistakes and poor decisions. Save it for after work, please.

Letting Little Kids Push the Cart

At least, if they're busy pushing the cart, they're not causing a scene. How many times do you find yourself maneuvering your cart through the aisle in such a way as to avoid an accident with a child? I see this more than I'd like.

In most cases, the child's view is obstructed by the cart; they push until they're told to stop, or they run into something. And they don't know how to position the cart when they stop.

They also don't know to stop at the end of the aisle and wait for an opening before leaving the aisle. (Of course, many adults don't know how to do this either.)

If you're going to let your child push the cart, use this time to educate them on proper etiquette. These lessons will serve them well in other situations beyond the grocery store.

Shoplifters

Oh, a five-finger discount? Have you ever witnessed a shoplifter? What do you do? Do you approach them, ignore them, or say something to an employee or manager?

Shoplifters are often masters of discretion, making it unlikely for you to catch them in the act. Their methods are diverse, from the basic pocketing of items to more sophisticated techniques—but this isn't a class on shoplifting,

Then there's the self-checkout shoplifting. The shoplifter will go through the motions, appearing to pay, and walk out of the store, leaving the next customer to pay for that purchase if they aren't paying attention. (To find out how I learned this, see "Self-Checkout.")

> **Did you know?** According to the National Retail Federation (NRF), U.S. retailers lost $112.1 billion to theft and other inventory shrinkage in 2022. That's mind-boggling! (Source: nrf.com)

Today, however, cameras are everywhere, and some stores have security people monitoring the cameras in real time.

All I can say is it's your call what you do if you see someone shoplifting. If you confront the shoplifter, there's always a risk of retaliation. I would, however, discreetly notify the manager or an employee.

Now, if a group is doing the shoplifting, I'd leave the area or even the store as this situation could escalate into something dangerous. Once you're safe, you can call the police.

Aggressive Charity Stands

Hey! Over here! How often do you use an alternate exit when you see a fundraiser table outside one of the entrances to the store?

I donate to multiple charities and almost always make it a point to go to these tables to see what they're doing, especially if there are children. The kids are delighted when someone comes to their table. And the fundraisers are generally for good causes. So, count me in.

However, some stands are overly aggressive, turning off potential donors. I know I'm not the only one who finds this counterproductive. Nobody likes to be coerced. The respectful approach is more effective.

This goes for aggressive vendors, too.

Sampling Fruit, Like Grapes

This isn't an open deli. It's always surprising to see someone reach into the grapes or berries and start eating. Maybe they're hungry and can't wait? Or they're trying them to see if they like them?

I don't care. If you want them, buy them.

And let's not forget, if these items are sold by weight and eaten throughout the store, it's not just a harmless act. It's theft, plain and simple.

Here's a good tip: Buy, leave the store, eat.

Sniffing Fresh Fruit or Vegetables

Mmmmm! I don't blame you for wanting to inhale the pleasant aroma of a ripe fresh tomato, and it's not a crime. After all, unlike baked goods, people can wash their fruit and vegetables when they get home.

However, sniffing and handling fruit and vegetables without purchasing them can spread disease. At least refrain from doing it if you're under the weather with something contagious. (In fact, try to avoid shopping entirely if that's the case; see also "Shopping While Sick.") And remember, others may have already touched those items before you.

If you want to check the firmness of a fruit or vegetable, consider using one of the plastic bags provided by the store as a glove.

Lastly, remember to thoroughly wash these unpackaged items at home before eating them.

No Cleaning Wipes at the Entrance

Be prepared! Since COVID-19 (2020–21), many stores provide cleaning wipes near the entrance. This is a great idea.

However, I'd like to respectfully ask stores to provide ample space to toss the used wipe; I've seen some dispensers with holes in the side the size of a silver dollar. Seriously. And then you see the used wipes lying all over the place.

It's a good idea to make sure you have your own wipes or hand sanitizer along with you—in case the store either doesn't provide them or is out of them. At least keep these things in your car. When I return to the car, I always use hand disinfectant.

You've still been handling items others have handled, such as the bags going into your house. There's no real way around this, but we can do our reasonable best to minimize the germs we pick up.

Narrow Aisles

Be like Costco! Why the narrow aisles? Well, the more space that can be used for products, the more products a store can offer. So, smaller aisles, more product.

While I understand the need for stores to maximize their space, it's important to acknowledge the frustration caused by narrow aisles. These aisles, where only one cart (or motorized cart) can fit, can be a major source of annoyance for shoppers.

The shopping experience, much like dining out, plays a pivotal role in determining whether a customer will return. If your shopping experience is less than desirable, it doesn't matter how many products the store has; they risk losing customers.

Costco's wide aisles and spacious carts provide a delightful shopping experience. Some aisles even allow four carts to move side by side, a stark contrast to the cramped aisles in many other stores.

A note here, however, that wider aisles don't always equate to proper use of carts. I sometimes find myself thinking, "And these people drive cars?"

But consider this: with wider aisles, more customers can be in the store simultaneously. So, the question is, would you rather have more products or more customers in your store at a time?

I suggest narrow-aisled stores seriously consider a change in aisle design. It's a choice that could increase your store's success.

Walking on Both Sides of the Aisles

Down the middle! You're strolling down the aisle, the path ahead clear, and suddenly, a shopper with a cartful of goods appears, heading straight towards you. So now you have them coming at you, along with someone else on the other side of the aisle coming at you. Great.

Just because we're buying products from both sides of the aisle doesn't mean we should move our cart down the middle of the aisle or from side to side.

During COVID, the grocery stores in my area put arrows on the floors to direct traffic in a one-way pattern through each aisle. At first, I found this awkward, but I soon saw it worked nicely. Despite some shoppers ignoring the arrows (much like they might disregard parking lot lines), the one-way system improved the shopping experience, making it much smoother and more organized.

The only drawback was going to an aisle where you needed something from the far end, and the direction of travel was against you.

A friend of mine told me how he got around this. He'd turn his cart around so that the cart was facing in the proper direction and then slowly move backward. While my friend's solution was indeed clever, I can't in good conscience recommend it!

In summary, always keep your cart to the right side of the aisle, as you'd do on the road. This follows common courtesy and ensures a smoother flow of traffic in the store.

Greeting Cards

A card for every occasion...if you can find them. If you want full-time employment, just ask for the job of maintaining greeting cards.

It would be handy if, say, all the anniversary cards were together. But they're often separated by companies rather than by occasion, so you must look at every brand's section to see all the anniversary cards.

I doubt half the shoppers return a card to the slot they got it from. Just like with magazines, the chances of a card being returned to its original slot are slim (see also "Reading Magazines and Newspapers Without Buying"). So we end up sifting through the cards in each slot, knowing they'll likely not all be the same.

It's not just the organization that's a problem. How many times have you found a card that's been bent or smudged from careless handling? And don't get me started on the envelopes. Some slots have ten, others none. It's like a game of luck.

And am I the only one who has noticed the price of greeting cards today? It's enough to consider the card the gift!

Reading Magazines and Newspapers Without Buying

If it's okay to read magazines without buying, is it okay to eat food and brush your teeth with a store toothbrush? A store isn't a library. You can scan through a magazine, but if you flat-out read it—and/or smudge or otherwise damage it—you should go ahead and buy it.

I can understand if you want to evaluate the content to see if it justifies the high magazine prices, but glance through, put it back or buy it, and move on.

And if you do put it back, please put it where and how you found it.

Store Music Selection, Quality, and Volume

It's beginning to look a lot like Christmas… It's enjoyable when a store plays pleasant and/or seasonal music on the store speaker system. Music, a subliminal element, can enhance the shopping experience, put us in a good mood, and potentially increase our purchases.

However, when the music selection isn't suitable for all customers, is too loud and jarring, or the system's quality creates discomfort, it disrupts the comfortable shopping environment a store aims to create.

Some stores will begin playing Christmas music in August, when most people aren't yet in the holiday spirit. This premature celebration, not to mention the aisles filled with Christmas decorations, can be off-putting to some customers. I'd start the Christmas music in November, right after Thanksgiving, which is more in line with the traditional holiday season.

But admittedly, there are some Christmas enthusiasts for whom it's never too early!

Employees Smoking by the Entrance

Smoke 'em if you got 'em! Don't you love walking into a store entrance and immediately being hit with stale cigarette smoke? Or finding employees standing there (usually on their phones) smoking? I didn't think so.

The first impression one gets when entering a store is lasting, and smoke odor detracts from that. And because the employees are smoking in an enclosed area, their clothes retain the smoke smell and carry it into the store. Overall, this shows a lack of consideration for customers.

To protect non-smokers from secondhand smoke, many states have laws that prohibit smoking (this also includes vaping and smokeless tobacco) within a certain distance of entrances/exits of public places and workplaces.

I'm not opposed to people smoking, but a good manager can find an appropriate place for employees to do that—if not in an out-of-the-way break room, maybe at the side of, or even behind, the building.

Going In the Exit and Out the Enter Doors

Are you coming or going? When you drive a car, do you look to see if a street is a one-way street? I'm guessing yes.

So why don't people look to see if the doorway is an entrance or an exit? Have you ever found yourself in the awkward situation of entering or leaving a store, only to face people coming from the wrong direction?

Have you ever been the one going the wrong way? I won't tell. I bet it was an honest mistake, an unfamiliar store.

This embarrassment can be avoided in the future by looking for signs on the doors. If there are separate exit/entrance doors, that will be indicated, and using the proper door will help prevent unnecessary confusion.

Customer Service Desk

Customer dis-service! Have you ever approached the customer service desk and found it unattended? I have, more than once.

The inconvenience of waiting, hoping for a service person to appear, only to have to track them down myself, is quite frustrating.

When they finally do show up, the least I hope for is a simple acknowledgment of the wait. A pleasant smile and greeting would be a bonus.

And another thing. When you're talking to the service person and the phone rings, do they continue to work with you or drop you like a sack of potatoes and answer the phone? If they answer the phone, they often focus on helping those people rather than putting them on hold. It's disappointing to see them prioritize phone calls over in-person customers. Hey, what about me?

Causing a Scene

Interesting personality! Some customers love to make a scene. Maybe it makes them feel important. They turn something simple into a crisis. I see these people and think I'm lucky not to work with or live near them, though I might watch them from a safe distance. I can't help but feel a surge of empathy for the employees in those situations.

A skilled employee will strive to defuse the situation and involve the manager if necessary. I've always admired the de-escalation skills of managers who, through their calm and composed demeanor, set the rest of us an excellent example for dealing with such characters.

Unsolvable Mysteries at the Checkout

This is gonna take a while! Sometimes, an issue arises during checkout that becomes an unsolvable mystery. It might be a new item like an odd sweet potato they can't figure out how to ring up, a coupon that doesn't scan (see also "Coupons Are Great, But…"), or the last of a discounted item no longer in the computer system.

So they insist on launching a deep investigation involving more senior cashiers—which seems to go nowhere as the line behind grows into a sea of packed shopping carts.

Whether you're right or wrong, instead of pushing the issue (for instance, if you're sure a coupon is still good but it doesn't register), it's more courteous to pay for everything else, then take the item in question to customer service to deal with it there. This way, you're not holding up an ever-growing line of impatient shoppers rolling their eyes and emitting deep sighs and groans.

Or else, there's always the option to quickly open up a couple more lanes for the other waiting customers while that lane continues solving the mystery.

Lousy Intercom System

Did you catch that? Remember the teacher in the Charlie Brown cartoons? Where she sounds like "Wah Wa Wa Wah Wa Wa" when she speaks? (I recommend these cartoons if you have yet to discover them.)

Some store intercoms sound the same way. Can anyone understand what's being said? Does anyone care?

The unclear intercom can lead to real problems if the announcement is an emergency or otherwise important information for customers. So why not take the trouble to get the intercom fixed?

Self-Checkout

Wow, that can't be my total! I was in a store a while back where I used the self-checkout. When I looked at the total, I realized there were some items on the list I hadn't purchased.

The previous person had scanned their items, gone through the motions of paying but not actually paid, and left.

I hadn't thought to look at the screen before scanning, and those items were combined with my purchases.

The manager hadn't realized the self-checkout was situated so the clerk at the regular checkout couldn't see the activity at the self-checkout station. This was soon rectified after my experience.

It made me wonder how many times this takes place daily.

Since then, I've seen more stores staffing the self-checkout area with employees who serve as monitors. This is good for catching people trying to steal, as well as guiding customers to open stations. These monitors also ensure the customer is at the correct register for cash or credit card.

Labels Facing Every Which Way

Hold on, let me fix that! Yep, you guessed it. I'm the guy walking through the stores turning products so labels are facing out.

As mentioned previously in this book, I have selective OCD (obsessive-compulsive disorder). At home, I always have to place labels out in the cupboard, refrigerator, and shelves.

I'll take this opportunity to share with you another OCD habit of mine. When I take products from the shelves, I pull forward the next product behind, so there's always one in the front.

I especially do this on the upper shelves where many people can't see anything beyond the first row. I know, I know. But I can't help myself!

While I understand this may seem like a small detail to some, I can't help but notice products on store shelves with labels not facing forward. If a store isn't doing this, I'm guessing there are other things they're not doing right.

This may seem petty to some of you, but it's the proper way to display products. The labels are there for two purposes. One is to help you identify a product quickly and easily. The other is to promote the product. A lot of time and money has gone into creating attractive labels to help you with your purchase.

So, the next time you see a product with the label facing in, you're welcome to join me. Maybe you'll turn the label out, too.

Cashier and Bagger Chatting

And what did your mother say? This is a common scenario when a cashier is conversing with the person bagging groceries or another fellow employee, and not engaging with the customer.

They might be discussing their previous or upcoming weekend or other personal matters that the customer isn't interested in hearing. In this situation, it feels like the customer is being ignored, as if they are interrupting the employees' conversation.

It's only fair that customers should come first during working hours, and they deserve that respect. What about catching up with your friend/coworker after the end of your shift, or at very least waiting until there's a lull with no shoppers at the register?

Camping Out to Study the Vitamin or OTC Section

Why not just pitch a tent? You stop by a familiar aisle to pick up a specific vitamin, supplement, or over-the-counter painkiller. You know just what you want; grabbing it will only take a minute.

Only someone is camped in front of the shelves, studying every bottle, scrutinizing the ingredients. Okay. You don't want to disturb them; you'll return to that aisle later, right before checkout. You have other items on your list, which should give them plenty of time.

But half an hour later, that customer is still hunkered down in the same spot. Now they've taken off their coat and have gotten out a notebook and a pen, and are writing things down, deep in concentration.

What should you do? Interrupt them? Skip getting your item and come back for it next week? Offer to bring them a chair?

These days, the Internet makes it easy to research comparable items beforehand and come prepared. But if we do need to spend an excessively long time in one section of shelves, it's considerate to frequently look around, to make sure other shoppers don't need to access something in that spot. And to go during off hours when it's not so busy.

Blocking the Exit or Aisle When Catching Up With an Old Friend

It's like you're the only two people in the world. It seems like synchronistic luck. If there's one person you're overjoyed to run into by chance, it's this old friend. It must have been eight years since you last saw each other, and you have so much catching up to do.

You're so absorbed in the conversation, you don't even realize you're blocking the exit—or the shelf of cookies another customer is eyeing.

I'm happy you got to reconnect. I only ask that you look for a spot away from customer traffic to enjoy your reunion. And I'll aim to do the same when this situation arises.

We used to live in a small town where everyone knew each other. A quick trip to the local store was anything but quick. You'd invariably run into familiar faces and take the time to exchange a few words, turning your brief errand into a long one.

Now that we live in a more populated area, it still amazes me how many people I recognize when I'm at the store. What are the odds?

People Who Are Too Chatty About What You're Buying

"Snacks…more snacks…more snacks…more snacks! Aren't you going to get anything good for you?"

It takes a pretty grumpy person to mind the occasional friendly remark from a fellow shopper or store employee about something in their cart. A simple, non-judgmental comment like "That looks good" or "I love those too" can be a pleasant exchange and brighten a person's day.

However, it's good not to go too far. Some may think it's harmless fun to, say, poke another shopper in the midsection after peering into their cart and yelling, "FOUR pork chops! Are you sure you need FOUR pork chops?" But such teasing can make many feel uncomfortable, as it can come across as invasive and overly familiar.

Even less extreme examples, like a cashier having something to say about every single item they ring up for you, can become tiresome ("Somebody sure likes peanut butter!"). Though I do think it would be interesting to be a cashier in a grocery store and see the types of products people buy.

Let's remember to respect personal boundaries and avoid making jokes or comments that could potentially embarrass a fellow shopper or customer, or make them feel awkward. When in doubt, don't.

No Money for Groceries

"It's taken care of." If you notice someone is stressed and struggling, counting change—and if you can afford it—go ahead and pay for their groceries. Or just do it randomly. I don't care if you do it anonymously or let them know you're doing it, use your own judgment. And thank you so much for your part in making the world a kinder, more generous place.

No Staff at the Bakery—Now What?

"I dunno, I think they're around a lot in the mornings…" You visit the bakery with the intention of placing a custom cake order for your friend's birthday, only to be met with untrained staff from other departments struggling to manage the bakery.

Despite offering custom orders, the bakery seems to lack a clear process or set hours for this service. However, you're aware of the bakery's reputation for delicious cakes, if only you could successfully place your order.

It's a bit of a nail-biter, not knowing if your cake will be ready for pickup on the big day. It's an adventure you didn't sign up for, but I guess you'll find out!

If clearly stated hours and a staffed bakery are sometimes too much to ask, easy-to-see directions for placing a custom order (maybe order sheets to fill out, in a tray on the counter?) might be the second-best solution. And a call from the bakery staff later to confirm your order would be nice too, so you know it was received and will be ready on time.

Digital Age Difficulties

Doesn't the computer do this for me? In this digital age, it's common (and understandable) to see cashiers who struggle with math because they rely on cash registers to do the calculations for them. When a customer hands them coins or bills different from what they're expecting, it throws them off.

In the past, it was common to see vendors at markets—like fruit and vegetable sellers—using a money box instead of a cash register. They'd calculate the total in their heads or on paper, collect the customer's money, and expertly count out the correct change into the customer's hand.

I encourage today's cashiers who grew up in the digital age to ask someone in their fifties or older who has experience with making change the traditional way to teach them this skill. You don't need to be a math genius; it only requires basic math. You'll also develop automatic good habits—such as sorting bills by denomination, all facing the same way—that will make you a better cashier as well as a more considerate shopper, regardless of technological advances.

And technology is evolving rapidly, as every year new methods of payment are introduced. Some stores now allow customers to scan items with their phones as they shop, enabling them to pay through their phones and exit via a security scan. Perhaps soon, facial recognition will become the standard for payment. Exciting times.

Items Falling Through Gaps in the Cart

Oh no, I lose so many jars of salsa this way! As you might know, especially if you're a parent, shopping carts with child seats have leg holes with flaps to cover them when not in use, to prevent smaller items from falling through the holes onto the floor.

What did you say? You never knew that was a child seat, but all this time thought it was just a handy shelf to hold the items you wanted to keep separate from the rest of your cart? Nope, Scout's honor, it really is a child seat—look it up online. Yep, a person learns something new every day.

Are you questioning the design of a cart that risks items falling through to the floor? I hear that. Maybe someday, a clever engineer will come up with a better one. In the meanwhile, though, it's good to get in the habit of checking your cart right away to see that the leg hole flap is securely in place and that there are no gaps or holes large enough for your jars of salsa to slip through.

Don't Open Me, Please!

Ooohhh, this deodorant smells good! I know this is an odd one, but I see this more than I'd like. Someone is opening a deodorant stick, a jar of fruit preserves, or even spaghetti sauce and smelling the contents. I know, I can't believe it either!

I understand the temptation to spray an air freshener to see how it smells, or to investigate that chocolate-swirled nut butter. However, as difficult as it might be to resist opening the lid for a closer inspection, please don't do it!

If, perish the thought, during some momentary shopping lapse, you absent-mindedly unscrew the lid of a jar to look at and/or sniff its contents (and in doing so, horrify any fellow shoppers who happen to witness this), please remember: if you open it, you must buy it.

Most containers have seals designed to protect the product from spoilage and contamination. If you break that seal and then decide to put the item back, there's a chance that the product, or the person who ultimately buys it, could be compromised.

So here's the deal: you open it, you buy it! This case (or jar) is closed!

Shopping While Sick

Aaaaachoo! Hey, what's your problem? Here's my problem. If you need an entire box of tissues for a trip to the grocery store, it's probably best to stay home. It's nice you want to share with others, but please don't!

Have you ever gone out to eat at a restaurant, only to have your appetite ruined by another diner's constant coughing and loud nose-blowing?

It's also unpleasant while shopping—whether it's someone sneezing all over the radishes or the person in front of you in the checkout line punctuating your wait with deep, rhythmic sniffles.

And then there's the cashier pushing through their shift with a cold, trying to make up for it with liberal use of hand sanitizer. (Employers, is it worth having your store fully staffed if it grosses out customers and potentially makes them sick?)

The recent COVID-19 pandemic has heightened people's caution for good reason.

The annoyance of listening to someone's cough or sniff is only overshadowed by the worry of catching their illness. The potential consequences of shopping while sick can be severe, even life-threatening. At the very least, it's frustrating for those who might end up sidelined by your cold for the next week.

We all share the responsibility to maintain a healthy environment in public spaces—which means staying home if we might be contagious, even if that inconveniences us.

However, there's a reason to give strangers the benefit of the doubt and refrain from glaring at them if they cough or sniffle in public. Not all coughs and sniffles indicate a contagious illness. Some people with non-contagious conditions, like Parkinson's, can't help it.

If you're sick, stay home until you're well. A friend might be willing to help by picking up some groceries for you.

Shopping Delivery Services

Where are they? Have you ever waited forever for groceries to be delivered, only to find out that some items are missing? Long delivery times are likely the top frustration for many customers. However, we should remember that using a delivery service saves us a trip to the store, and nobody's perfect.

Like food delivery, grocery delivery service is increasingly common and seems to be here to stay. While most grocery delivery services operate independently of grocery stores, they still represent those stores.

I know you want to treat your grocery delivery person right, so here are a few suggestions to that end:

- Unlike package delivery drivers, grocery delivery personnel rely on and appreciate tips. And deserve them, too, for saving us a trip to the grocery store. A generous tip is especially warranted if they handle your items with care and follow your instructions.
- Take the time to make sure your directions are clear and easy to follow. Have you ever tried to follow confusing directions? It's frustrating.
- Keep your pets are contained so they can't harass or threaten the delivery person.
- Be considerate of delivery people working in inclement weather. Please don't ask them to drive up icy hills. In winter, shovel your driveway and take any necessary precautions (like spreading ice melt or salt) to prevent them from slipping and falling.

Let's remember that having grocery delivery service is a privilege. Delivery people aren't robots; they have feelings, and deserve our respectful and considerate treatment.

Handbaskets

Now *I'm* a basket case! How often have you gone to the store to get one or two items only to find yourself at the back of the store with an armload of stuff? Yeah, I thought so.

Now, you begin looking for a stack of handbaskets, only to find none. Most places have these baskets at the entry, but I wish every store would strategically place them throughout the store for people like me (and maybe you?).

I used to find myself in this predicament, but now I grab a full-size shopping cart upon entering the store. I probably get more than I intend (maybe this is why some stores don't have handbaskets throughout the store), but at least I'm not performing a juggling act for those around me. Hmm... that might be entertaining!

So, think ahead, or stick to your one or two items.

Closing Time

But I'm not done yet? Hey, did you know that the store closes at a certain time for a reason? It's not just a suggestion. But some people seem to think they can stroll in five minutes before closing and take their sweet time filling a cart. It's not fair to the employees who are ready to go home.

The store employees are turning out the lights and shooting them nervous glances.

Yet, these late shoppers act entitled like, well I'm here, so you have to take care of me, you can't turn away a customer.

If it's ten minutes before closing time and you want to run in and get one or two items, that's one thing. But I've really seen people try to push this. The manager or workers have to come to the person and plead with them to stop shopping.

It's not just about the closing time, it's about the workers' need for rest and time with their families. Let's not keep them from their well-deserved dinner.

Tips for Courteous and Friendly Shopping

To summarize everything you've read, here's a checklist of things to consider when going to the store:

- When entering and leaving the parking lot, keep your eyes open for pedestrians and park between the lines.
- When entering the store, move through the entrance to where you can step to the side to check your list and plan.
- Keep your cart to the right side of the aisle or, as necessary, dictated by other cart traffic.
- If you need to leave your cart, leave it in a way that isn't obstructing others.
- If you decide you don't want something you've put in your cart, return it to where you got it.
- Be considerate of others' space.
- Stay off your phone unless it's an emergency or you're reading your list.
- Look both ways when leaving and entering an aisle.
- Patiently wait your turn at the deli and checkout.

- Be kind and respectful to others, and help those who may need it.
- Place your items in the proper order on the belt.
- Say "thank you" to the cashier and the person who bags your purchases.
- Return your cart to the store or cart return.
- Streamline your shopping experience by by organizing your shopping list the way the store is laid out—so you can efficiently go from one aisle to the next, rather than randomly zigzagging all around the store.
- Check your receipt to make sure you paid the price advertised on the shelf. Not all stores keep their prices up to date in their systems.
- Sat "thank you" to veterans, police officers, and Rescue.
- If there is a BOGO (Buy One Get One) and you don't need two, go ahead and get two and donate the second item to a food shelter, veterans organization, or church.

Thank you.

Afterword

I hope you enjoyed shopping with me and discovering the many irregular shopping behaviors and situations that can occur in stores.

After reading this book, I hope you have a better understanding of the negative and disrespectful behaviors people sometimes display while shopping, how to avoid them, and what steps to take if you encounter them.

As I mentioned earlier (and it's worth repeating because it's important!), please take a moment to reflect on your own habits and consider what you might improve.

Thank you for reading this book. I look forward to seeing you at the store! And when I do, thank you for not…

Shopping Me Crazy!

About the Author

John Reinhardt has been designing books for 49 years with thousands of books to his credit. This is his second book as an author.

John lives in a golf community in central Florida with his wife, Lynn. When he is not designing books or writing, he spends his time playing golf, gardening, brewing, target shooting, creating things, playing guitar, shooting pool, and just about anything else there is to do.

John enjoys shopping at grocery stores. Always fascinated with human behavior, when traveling he visits stores to study package design and look for unique products not found at his local stores.

You can contact John at:
DesignerofBooks@gmail.com

For updates and information:

www.YoureDrivingMeCrazy.com

If you enjoyed this book, you'll want to read...

**Available on Amazon
and online bookstores!**

Check out www.youredrivingmecrazy.com
for information about other books
in the CRAZY! series.

www.ingramcontent.com/pod-product-compliance
Lightning Source LLC
Chambersburg PA
CBHW060330050426
42449CB00011B/2714